Richard Despard Dodge

The Dodge Lands at Cow Neck

An Appendix to Robert Dodge's History of Tristram Dodge

Richard Despard Dodge

The Dodge Lands at Cow Neck
An Appendix to Robert Dodge's History of Tristram Dodge

ISBN/EAN: 9783337231996

Printed in Europe, USA, Canada, Australia, Japan

Cover: Foto ©ninafisch / pixelio.de

More available books at **www.hansebooks.com**

THE DODGE LANDS AT COW NECK,

AN

APPENDIX

TO ROBERT DODGE'S

HISTORY OF TRISTRAM DODGE

AND HIS

DESCENDANTS IN AMERICA,

—BY—

RICHARD DESPARD DODGE.

PREFACE.

The errors and omissions inevitably occurring in the first edition of any work, and especially in a Genealogy, where absolute accuracy is difficult of attainment, led the writer to construct a list of errata in his own copy of the above History ; additions of new matter were made, and the result was finally embodied in the ensuing pages, which naturally fall into three divisions, as follows :—

Part I.—Corrections to be made in the first edition of the History.

Part II.—Description of the "Dodge Lands" at Cow Neck, L. I.

Part III.—Reminiscences of the Old Dodge Homestead, at Port Washington, by Henry T. Dodge.

Although some parts of this Appendix are of necessity rather "dry," yet there are several quaint and interesting items which it is hoped will be found acceptable to the members of our family, and perhaps even to the general reader.

Valuable assistance has been given in this work by the following relatives and friends: Robert Dodge, the author of the "History"; Henry O. Dodge, and his son Henry T. Dodge, of Port Washington, L. I.; Mrs. Helen D. Campman, of New York, and H. M. W. Eastman, Esq., of Roslyn; to all of whom grateful acknowledgments are due.

Brooklyn, January, 1896.

CONTENTS.

PART I.—CORRECTIONS TO BE MADE IN THE FIRST
EDITION OF THE HISTORY PUBLISHED IN 1886.

On page 12, line 4, for "followers," read "companions."
   "   "   38, last line, for 1684, read 1690.
   "   "   41, line 3, for children, read child.
   "   "   42, line 4, for 1821, read 1810.
   "   "   42, line 6, for 1684, read 1690.
   "   "   42, line 18—The tombstone mentioned is marked
T. D. 1789 and is therefore *not* that of Thomas, Senior,
who died July 19, 1755, but of his son Thomas, Jr.
who dropped dead between the house and the barn
on May 12, 1789.
On page 43, 4th line from bottom, read Henry Onderdonk
Dodge.
On page 44, 8th line from bottom, read Herbert K. Dodge,
who married Nov. 14, 1894, Gertrude E. Edmonds.
On page 44, after fifth line from bottom, insert—Henry
Thomas Dodge married at Poughkeepsie, N. Y.,
April 16, 1884, Marie Antoinette Polhemus ; child,
Charles Forster Dodge, b. June 19, 1886.
On pages 44, 45 and 59—The Tristram Dodge mentioned
here must not be confounded with the grandson of
the first settler of Block Island, referred to on page
41 at top of page, and also on page 56; he was doubt-
less a descendant of the first Tristram, and on pages
22 and 25 of this appendix the probabilities of his
being a son of Jeremiah are considered.
On page 57, line 11, for Gen. I., read Geo. I.
On page 57, line 16, erase first figure 2, so as to read "Lib.
2 p. 395."
On page 58, line 8, for John, read Joshua.
On page 60, line 14, for 1766, read 1761.
On page 98, lines 3 and 4, should be omitted.
On page 119, line 6, for 1766 read 1761.

———————

On page 121, in place of the first few lines of the following poem as given there, insert the whole as follows:
It should be read twice, the first time reading each
line straight across; the second time, reading the first
half of two lines, and then the second half of the same two,
and so on.

(Written by Samuel Dodge, Jr., son of Samuel of Cow Neck, and great grandson of the first Tristram Dodge of Block Island, he being a member of the New York Legislature at the time)

"THE POLITICAL SENTIMENTS OF THE AUTHOR, 1779."

Hark! hark! the trumpet sounds— The din of War's alarms
O'er seas and solid grounds, Do call us all to arms.
Who for King George do stand, Their honors soon will shine,
Their ruin is at hand, Who with the Congress join.
The acts of Parliament, In them I much delight,
I hate their curst intent, Who for the Congress fight.
Who non resistance hold, They have my hand and heart,
May they for slaves be sold. Who act a Whiggish part.
The Tories of the day, They are my daily toast,
They soon shall sneak away. Who independence boast.
The Congress of the States, I hate with all my heart,
Blessing upon them waits, Who e'er take Britain's part.
To General Washington Confusion and dishonor,
May numbers daily run To Britain's royal banner.
On Mansfield, North and Bute May daily blessings pour
Confusion and dispute, On Congress evermore.
To North, that British Lord, May honors still be done,
I wish a block, or cord, To General Washington.

On page 122, lines 15 and 16—Erase statement that Samuel Dodge was a member of the Cincinnati.
On page 123, line 10, for 1842 read 1847.
"   "   125, 3d line from bottom, for 1842 read 1847.
"   "   126, line 4, for John read Jane.
"   "   129, line 12, for 1795 read 1797.
"   "   129, line 14, for 1798 read 1790.
"   "   130, line 7 from bottom, for 29, read 27.
"   "   131, line 2, for 1835 read 1853.
"   "   133, line 7, for 1867 read 1864.
"   "   133, replace lines 8 to 13, by the following list of the descendants of Daniel Dodge—Son of the above Samuel Dodge, Jr.

7

Children of Daniel and Ann Dodge.

1. Jane,   b. 156 William St., N. Y., May 29, 1797.   d. May 10, 1799
2. Jane,   b. at Poughkeepsie, N. Y., Sept 23, 1799.   d. Aug. 17, 1821.
3. Ann Eliza, b. 374 (now 378) Pearl St., N. Y., Nov. 21, 1801. d. Oct. 16, 1889.
4. Sarah Addoms,   Jany. 19, 1804.   d. Jan. 23, 1845.
5. Richard James,   Jany. 26, 1807.   d. Aug 2, 1891.
6. Emeline Amanda,   Feb 10, 1809.   .
7. Helen,   June 30, 1811.   d Mar. 30, 1823.
8. Susan   } twins,   Nov. 18, 1813   d. Sept. 28, 1813.
9. William, }   Nov. 18, 1813   d. Sept 20, 1814.
10. Mary Catharine,   May 23, 1816.   d Sept. 73, 1826.
11. Susan Augusta,   Aug 29, 1819.

Ann Eliza Dodge m. Dec. 20, 1825, Wm Ward Wheeler, who d. Jan. 2, 1871.

CHILDREN.

1. Jane Dodge Wheeler, b Dec. 20, 1826. d Nov 1, 1895.
2. Julia Eliza W., b.   { m. Edmund W. Blinn.
                  { Children—William,
                  { Jennie Louise. m. Oct. 15, 1895
3. Mary Louisa W., b.   { m. Clifford A. Baker. She d. July 2, 1867.
                  { 1 child, Mary Celestia.
4. Richard James W., b.   d.
5. Richard Oakley W., b Dec. 14, 1834   m. Dec. 16, 1863, Amelia Seymour.
6. Ann Augusta W., b.   1837 ? m.   Wm. Adams.
                     { Charles W.,
            Children { Richard,
                     { William.
7. Wm. Sam'l Packer W., b. Mar. 11, 1839. m.
                     { Wm. Ward,
            Children { Chas. Frederick,
                     { Blanche.
8. Chas. Frederick W., b. June 28, 1842. d. July 27, 1866.

Sarah Addoms Dodge m. July 2, 1833, Peter C. Oakley ; d. Jan. 13, 1842.

Susan A. Dodge, m. April 16, 1844. Richard B. Despard, b. June 26, 1809.

R. J. Dodge, m. (1). Nov. 16, 1837, Henrietta Despard,(sister of R. B. Despard.)
b. Feb. 24, 1813,
d. May 26, 1874.

m (2). Nov. 7, 1877, Jane Ann Andrews, b. Mar. 6, 1824.

Children of Richard James and Henrietta Dodge.

Richard Despard, b Sept. 6, 1839.
m. July 19 1866, Annie W. Nourse. b. June 2, 1845. d. Mar. 13, 1870.

Children { Francis Despard, b. Jan. 14, 1868. m. Apr 18, 1895, Ella B. Patterson
Richard Joseph, b. Mar. 11, 1870. d. Sept. 13, 1871.

Francis Edward, b. Mar. 3, 1841.
m. (1) Feb. 13, 1866, Matilda B. Cumming. b Jan. 14, 1848. d May 5, 1872.

Children—1. Edith Matilda. b. Apr. 3, 1867. d. May 17, 1872.
2. Isabella Despard b. Oct. 5, 1868. d Apr. 2, 1872.
3 Margaretta Bach Cumming. b. Feb. 3, 1871.
m (2) Oct. 19, 1876, Magdalen Talmage. b. Nov. 3, 1854.

Children—4. Helen. b. Jan. 3, 1878
5. Dorothea Miller. b, June 26. 1880. d. Dec. 24,'82.
6. Francis Talmage. b. Feb. 25, 1882.
7. Lyndon. b. Nov. 28, 1885.

3. Jane Isabella. b Jan. 21, 1843. d. Mar. 5. 1844.

4. Henrietta Leonora. b. May 23, 1845 d. Jan. 19, 1877.
m. July 17, 1866, Charles McMillan.

Children—1. Charles Richard. b. May 8, 1868. m. Feb., 1895.
2. Augusta Clementina. b. Feb. 19 1871.
3. Henry Lyndon b. 1874.

5 Augusta Clementina (twin sister of Henrietta) b. May 23, 1845. d. Nov. 3. 1869.

6. Anna Rosalie. b. Apr. 27, 1847. d, Apr. 16, 1849.

7. Edmund Arthur. b. July 7, 1850. m. Sept. 8, 1886. Caro F. Burwell.

8. Wm Wheeler. b. Aug. 18, 1854. m. Apr. 18, 1888. Jeannie V. Jones
Child—Mildred. b. Jan. 30, 1890.

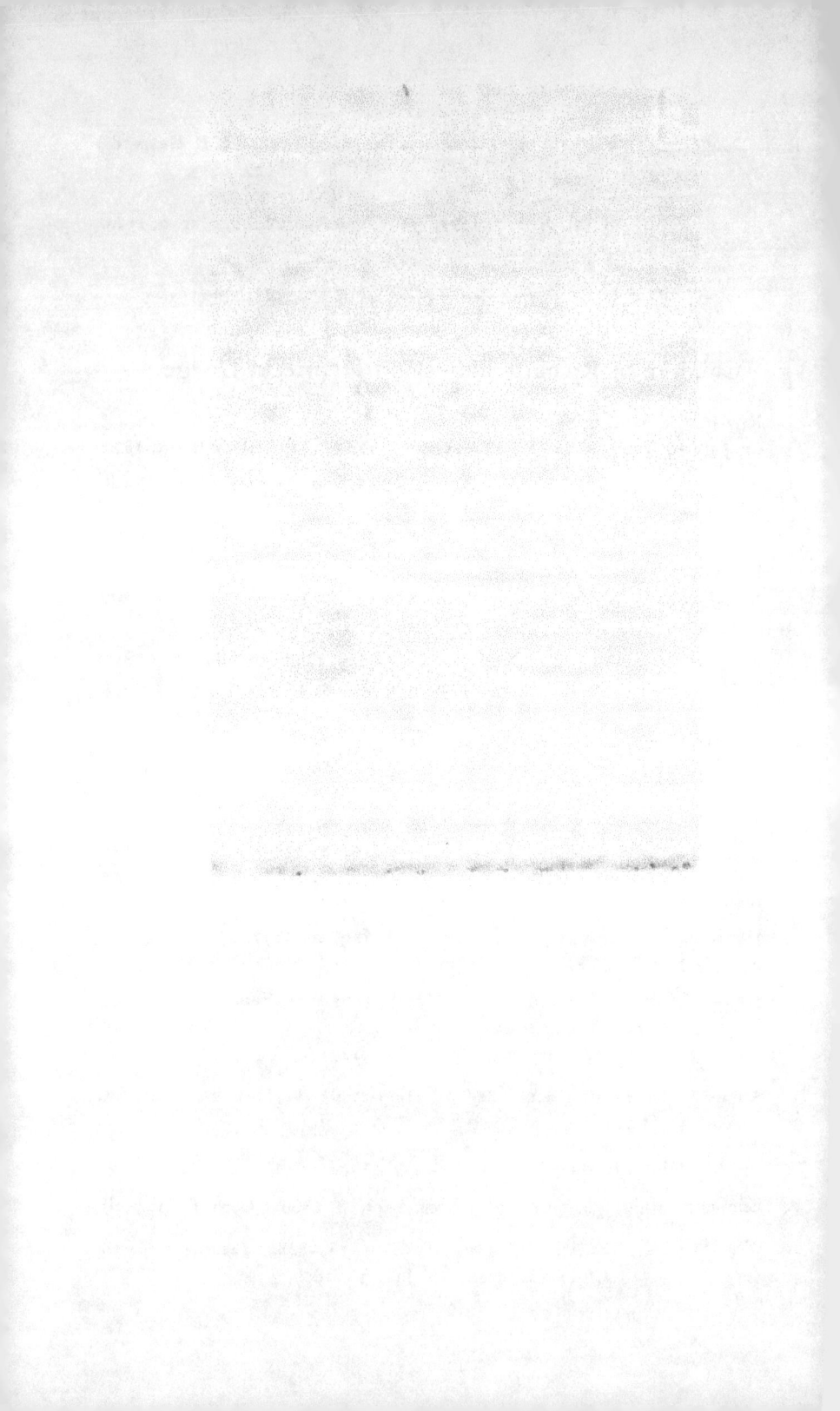

Daniel Dodge inherited his father Samuel's poetical talent, and was a man of refined tastes and especially skilful in vocal music. He was born in New York, December 14, 1764, probably at the old family homestead, No. 374 Pearl St. (now 378.) He resided there, with the exception of an interval at Poughkeepsie, for more than sixty years; although not always in the same house, as the original building was destroyed during the Revolution. He served during the War of 1812, and for many years afterwards, as Colonel of one of the New York State Regiments, and Brigadier-General. After spending almost a lifetime in the U. S, Government service in the New York Custom House, he with many others of the wrong political stripe, was removed from office by Andrew Jackson.

His son, Richard J. Dodge, was likewise gifted with natural aptitude for poetry and music, combined with business capacity. At the age of fourteen he entered the employ ment of Bach & Bradish, of 43 Fulton St., New York, Importers of Drugs and Chemicals. On the dissolution of this firm in the year 1841, he formed a co-partnership with Thomas W. Cumming, son-in-law of Robert Bach, the senior partner, as their successors. The business was continued under the various firm names of George D. Phelps & Dodge (1848), Dodge & Colvill (1850), Dodge, Colvill & Olcott (1859), and finally Dodge & Olcott (1861), who for many years have been established at 86 & 88 William St., N. Y. He was, therefore, at the time of his death, the head of a mercantile house that had been in existence for at least ninety-three years, during seventy of which years he had been connected with it; and by his ability and integrity he had been instrumental in building it up to a large measure of influence and prosperity. In 1840 he changed his residence from New York to Brooklyn, becoming there a citizen widely known for benevolence and good works. In 1848 he united with the First Presbyterian Church on Henry St., and at the time of his death he had been one of its Ruling Elders for thirty-three years, a long period of consistent Christian example.

On page 133, bottom line, add " died 1886."

On page 137, 9th line from bottom, for 1727 read 1707.

On page 140, line 3, erase "at eighteen."

On page 142, lines 8 and 9 should read thus : " His son, the Hon. Henry Dodge, fitly began in the wilderness, a life which," etc.

On page 219, line 14, for "a half mile " read "three."

On page 230, 3d line from bottom, for 1684 read 1690.

On page 231, line 5, for I. G. Clowes read Samuel Clowes.

On page 231, line 6, erase "by the name of West's Patent."

On page 231, line 8, read "mill-pond of Cornell."

On page 231, line 14. The conveyance here referred to is on record at Jamaica, in Liber 440, page 63, and is given later in this appendix (on page 16.)

On page 231, line 6 from bottom, for " westerdly " read " northerdly."

On page 231, line 4 from bottom, for "northerdly" read " southerdly."

On page 231, line 2 from bottom, for "prior to" read "in."

On page 232, lines 1 and 2 should be " Thomas made his first purchase of land early in 1718, from Samuel Clowes."

Insert here between lines 2 and 3, " Thomas purchased the farm now occupied by his great grandson Henry Onderdonk Dodge and family, from Joshua Cornell in 1721, (as more fully appears later on page 18 of this.)

On page 232, line 7. This date of 1684 is in conflict with the date in the Family Bible of Thomas Dodge, senior, (now in possession of Henry O. Dodge) which gives June 23, 1690, as the date of his birth.

On page 232 omit lines 12, 13, 14 and 15.

Note at foot of page 233. There are several old private grave-yards of the Dodge family at Cow Neck. One is near the lane, just above the former homestead of Joseph Dodge and his son, Isaac H. Dodge, now occupied by Jesse H. Bunnell. Another is near the southerly line of property now in possession of Elbert Bogart, on the west shore of Hempstead Harbor. It contains several primitive gravestones, the inscriptions on very few of them being legible ; of these, two are marked W. D., 1767, and I. D., 1778, supposed to belong to William Dodge and Joseph Dodge, sons of Thomas and Tristram respectively, of the original settlers at Cow Neck.

PART II.—THE DODGE LANDS AT COW NECK.

These were on the west side of Hempstead Harbor, directly opposite. Sea Cliff, L. I., having a front of three-quarters of a mile on the shore, and running back across the Neck about a mile and a half to Port Washington, on Manhasset Bay, formerly Cow Bay. In order to locate them with accuracy, it is necessary to begin with an examination of the ancient Map of the Division of the Common Lands, made by Samuel Clowes. (See page 231 of the History.) The original map is now in the possession of Henry T. Dodge, of Port Washington, but it is in a very dilapidated condition, both on account of its age, and from being made on ordinary white drawing paper, in place of stronger material. The title of the map is as follows:

"A map of a Survey of that part of Cow Neck which be-
"longs to the Gate-right men, done by order of John Sands
"and Jonathan Smith, pursuant to powers granted them by
"the persons concerned in a Writing dated 16—8 ber, 1695.
"Begun ye 30th March, 1703, and thus finished ye 17th of
"ffebruary, 1709.
                  "BY SAMUEL CLOWES, Surveyor."

A copy of this map was made in 1745, on parchment, which is now in the possession of H. M. W. Eastman, Esq., of Roslyn, L. I. On this copy is written the following:

"Whereas, the Mapp of the Survey of that part of Cow
"Neck which belongs to ye Gate-right men, formerly made
"by Samuel Clowes, Surveyor, being much defaced and
"likely to be Extinguished if not timly Remodeled; there-
"fore, in order to Revive and Continue ye same, ye Pro-
"prietors of ye lands Contained within ye aforesaid Mapp
"have agreed with me to draw a new Draught from ye
"Original Conformable to their agreement, I have ex-
"tracted this figure from ye Original Map, and as nearly
"agreeing with ye former as I could (with care and Dili-
"gence) Perfect it.
                  "Performed by me,
                        "SAMUEL WILLIS, Surveyor.
"Ye 12th of 2 mo.
    "Anno Domini, 1745."

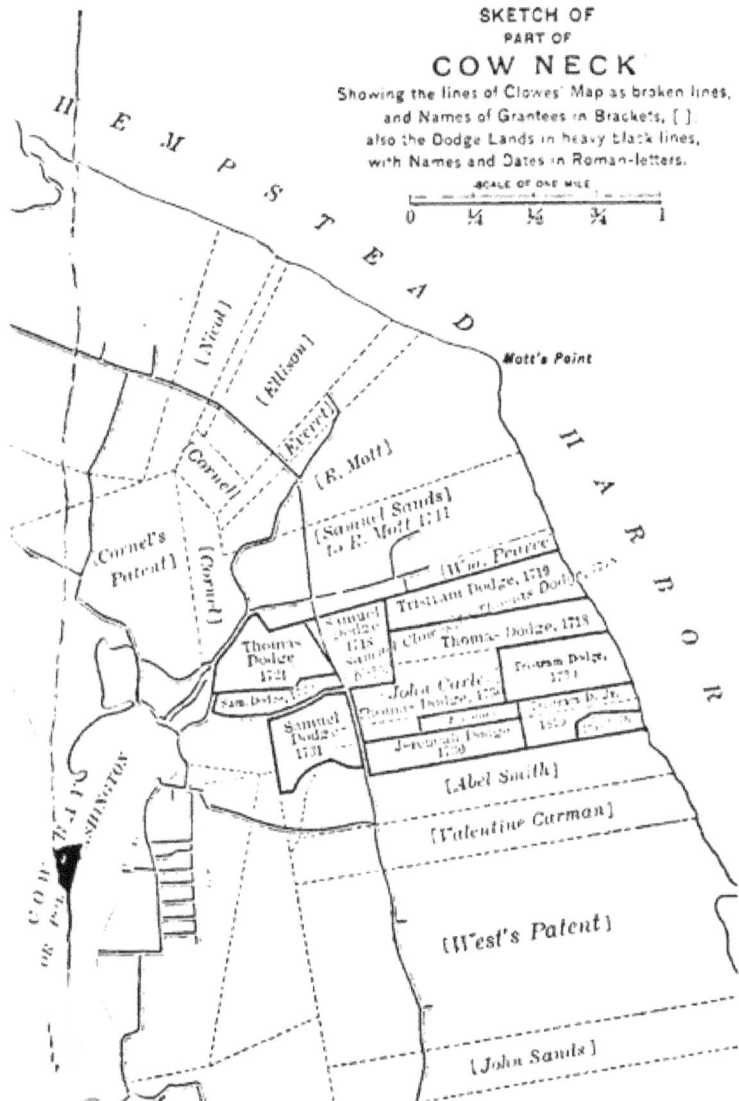

SKETCH OF
PART OF
COW NECK
Showing the lines of Clowes' Map as broken lines,
and Names of Grantees in Brackets, [ ].
also the Dodge Lands in heavy black lines,
with Names and Dates in Roman-letters.

SCALE OF ONE MILE

0   ¼   ½   ¾   1

H E M P S T E A D

Mott's Point

H A R B O R

(Nicol)

(Ellison)

(Everett)

(R. Mott)

(Cornel)

(Samuel Sands)
to R. Mott 1711

Cornel's
Patent)

(Cornel)

Wm. Pearce

Tristram Dodge, 1719

Samuel   Clowes Dodge,
Dodge
1718   Thomas Dodge, 1718

Thomas
Dodge
1731   Samuel
Dodge

Sam. Dodge   John Carle
Thomas Dodge, 1735   Tristram Dodge,
1731

Samuel   Thomas D. Jr.
Dodge
1731   Jeremiah Dodge

C O W   B A Y

W A S H I N G T O N

(Abel Smith)

(Valentine Carman)

(West's Patent)

(John Sands)

Both the original map and the copy were on a scale of 16¾ chains to an inch. A sketch of Cow Neck is given on the preceding page, on which a reproduction of the principal part of the old map on a smaller scale is shown, the broken lines being the division lines of the allotments. The names of some of the original grantees appear in brackets [ ], and in briefer form than on the old map. The boundaries of the Dodge lands are denoted by heavy black lines, and the names and dates are in Roman letters.

It appears from the records that Thomas Dodge purchased the allotment of Samuel Clowes (the Surveyor himself) in 1718, and he then sold part of it to his cousin Samuel, and part to his brother Tristram. Afterwards, he bought the present homestead farm, which has descended in a direct line to his great grandson, Henry O. Dodge; and later, in 1730, he acquired part, if not the whole, of the allotments of Carle & Ellison, on Clowes' map.

Samuel Dodge, in addition to the farm received from Thomas Dodge, purchased from Joshua Cornel the tract lying between the above mentioned homestead farm and the "Sandy Hollow Road." He next bought, in 1731. 53¾ acres from Andrew Onderdonk, on the southeast corner of said "Sandy Hollow Road" and the "Middle Neck Road;" and also at some time unknown, but before 1730, a ten acre lot, south of the plot obtained from Thomas Dodge in 1718.

In 1711, before the appearance of the above members of the Dodge family at Cow Neck, Samuel Sands sold his allotment to Richbell Mott, as recorded at Jamaica in Liber C, page 52, and it is this tract that is mentioned in the deed from Samuel Clowes to Thomas Dodge, as bounding the property on the north.

The following is a more detailed narrative of the various early purchases, together with the corresponding descriptions in the deeds, etc.

1—Samuel Clowes, of Jamaica in Queens County, on the Island Nassau, Gent. and Catharine his wife, of the one part ; and Thomas Dodge, of Hempstead, in the County aforesaid, Yeoman.

Deed dated Feb. 18, 1718, " in " the 5th year of the reigne " of our soveraigne Lord " King George, &c. in the " year of Man's Salvation, " 1718."

Consideration 373 pounds, 14 shillings and 3 pence, lawful money of New York. Conveys " All that his ye " said Samuel Clowes' certain " farm, plantation or tract of " land, situate, lying and be- " ing on Cow Neck, in the Township of Hempstead and " County abovesaid, containing 202 acres and a quarter and " 14 square roods; being bounded easterly by Hempstead " Harbor ; northerly, partly by Richard Greave and partly " by Richbell Mott : westerly, by other lands laid out upon " gate-rights; and southerly, by the land belonging to the " heirs of John Carle, deceased. Excepting and always re- " serving out of this present grant * * the full quantity " of 20 acres of land to be cutt off on that side of said tract " lying next adjacent to the land now in the possession of " Richard Greave aforesaid, to be 20 roods in breadth at the " waterside, and at the other end to begin at the great wal- " nut tree which stands in a southwest corner of the said " Richard Greaves, and to run thence southerly so far as to " contain and take in the said quantity of 20 acres. Only " the said Thomas Dodge, his heirs and assigns, to have the " liberty (for a convenient place to be appointed by the said " Samuel Clowes or his heirs and assigns) of a cartway over " the said 20 acres of land, and also the liberty of using the " Spring that is thereon, if. they have occasion, they taking " care to put up the bars. To have and to hold, etc.

S. CLOWES [L. S.]
CATHARINE CLOWES [L. S.] "

Acknowledged Feb. 12, 1723-4.
Recorded June 10, 1874, in Liber 440, page 63, at Jamaica

Nothing further has been found in regard to the above reservation of 20 acres; it was probably acquired later by Thomas Dodge or his heirs and assigns.

2—Thomas Dodge, and Susannah, his wife, of Hempstead, Queens Co., Province of New York, Yeoman; to Samuel Dodge of the same place, Yeoman.

Deed dated March 18, 1718. (Recorded Liber 2, page 395.) Consideration £124. Conveys "Farme att Hemp-" stead of 59 acres and 26 " square rods, or one-third, " lacking Five acres of that " Farme that was Samuel " Clowes'; bounded Easterdly " partly by Thomas Dodge " aforesaid, and partly by Tristram Dodge, and northerdly " by Rigbell Mott; westerdly by other lands laid out upon " gate-rights, and Southerdly by land belonging to the heirs " of John Carle, deceased."

Witnessed by Thomas; (Jr.), Wilkie and Tristram Dodge. (A copy of the above deed is in the History, page 57.)

3—Thomas Dodge to Tristram Dodge. (See page 231 of the History, where the date is given as Jan. 11, 1719.) No record has yet been found of the sale of this plot of 79 acres to Tristram Dodge.

4—Capt. Joshua Cornel of Cow Neck in town-ship of Hempstead, Queens Co., Province of New York, to Samuel Dodge, of same place, Yeoman.

" Maid ye 17th March 1720. (Lib. 2 p. 397.) Consider-ation Fifty Pounds. Conveys " a certain Messuage or dwel-" ling house with the land the " said house stands on, at " Cow Neck, nigh Collard's " Cove, with a certain tract of " land nigh adjoining to the " said house, butted and " bounded as followeth: Beginning at a stake standing to " the North of a Black Oak tree, it being Thomas Carle's " corner tree, thence southardly by Carle's land to a black " oak stump on the north of the road; thence westerly to " another black oak stump, being formerly Collard's bound

17

"tree; so still running westerly to a post and rail fence now
"standing, so westerly as fence now runs, to the road;
"thence northerly as fence now runs to a stake by the fence;
"thence easterly as fence now runs to another stake; thence
"northeasterly to stake we first begin at; being by compu-
"tation 20 acres more or less.

"Also I do further grant all my right, title, interest,
"etc., to All the commons or unenclosed lands adjoining to
"the aforesaid tract of land lying on the south and west
"side of the above named fence."

(See page 58 of History.)

5.—Josuah Cornel of Cow Neck, &c., and Sarah, his wife, to Thomas Dodge, of same place, Yeoman.

Deed dated July 4, 1721. (Not recorded.) Consideration £144, 7s, 6d.
Conveys, "All, &c., on Cow "Neck. Begin at a Redd "Oak tree, by a path that "goes across the Neck, it "runs N 33° E 13 roods to
"another redd oak tree, thence East 28° North 14 roods to
"a small walnut standing by a brook, thence S. 26° E. 28
"roods to another small walnut, thence East 10° N. 45¾ roods
"to a large white oak, thence S 33° W."—(Error in deed. This
"should be S 33° E.)--"74 roods to a black oak standing by
"another path that goes along the Neck, thence west 3°
"south 44 roods to a stake, thence west 50° south 10¾
"roods to another stake, thence due west 103¼ roods to
"first mentioned path or highway, thence northerly along
"said path till it comes to the first station. Containing 53¾
"acres. Bounded westerly by first mentioned path and
"other land of said Josuah Cornel, northerly by Edmond
"Mott, easterly and southerly by Samuel Dodge."

This is the farm now occupied by Henry O. Dodge and family.

6—By reference to the next description (No. 7, below), we find that Samuel Dodge was in possession before 1730, of a "ten acre lot," directly south of his first purchase from Thomas Dodge. The conveyance of this lot has not yet been found in the records.

7—*A tract of 81 acres belonging to Thomas Dodge*, being part of the Carle & Ellison allotments on Clowes' map. No record has been found of this, but the following description is copied from a Diagram of the Survey of said 81 acres, now among the papers of H. T. Dodge.

"On ye 31th day of March 1730, atte The Request "of Thomas Dodge of Cow Neck, in the Bounds of Hemp-"stead in Queens County on Long Island, I have measured "and Laid to Thomas Dodge aforesaid, a certain tract or "Royal of Land lying on Cow Neck aforesaid, containing "81 acres, 3 roods, 27 rods. The first Bounder is the south-"west corner of Samuel Dodge's Ten Acres, which he "bought Thomas, which Thomas Dodge bought with his "own land of Rem Remsen; so ranging along the east side "of the highway S. 14° E. 10 chains 90 links to a black oak "tree, stand on the East side of the Highway, thence S. 9° "E. 5 chains to Jeremiah Dodge's northwest corner. Rang-"ing as Jeremiah's land runs, E. 2° N. 20 chains to a stake "to Andrew's southwest corner of his 20 acre lot, thence N. "9° W., 5 chains to Andrew's northeast corner, thence as "his land runs E. 2° N., 29 chains to Trustrim Dodge's "southwest corner to a stake, thence N. ¼° E., 16 chains 8 "links, thence upon a Strate line to Samuel's northeast cor-"ner of his ten acres, thence S. 2½° E. 5 chains, 93 links, and "then as Samuel's Line Runs to the place of beginning.
"Performed by me.
"SAM'L WILLIS."

8—Andrew Onderdonk of Cow Neck, Hempstead, Queens Co., Prov. N. Y., Yeoman and Greetry, his wife,

to

Samuel Dodge of the same place, Yeoman.

Deed dated 12th April, 1731. Recorded Lib. 2 p. 392. Consideration £274, 12s. Conveys "one piece, etc. of 'land on Cow Neck, etc. "Butted and bounded as "follows: Easterly by High-"way that leads through y^e "Neck; northerly by the "Highway that leads to "Landing, westwardly by land "of Robert Hutchings and "Jonathan Whitehead. "southerly by land of "Andrew Onderdonk, aforesaid: Beginning at a White Oak 'sapling, standing by the roadside, it being Robert Hutch-"ings' northeast corner tree, running thence S. 1¼° west, 24 "chains and 53 links, to a stake; thence east 2½° south, 2 "chains; thence east 6° south, 2 chains and 34 links; thence "N., 17° E. 2½ chains; thence N. 30° E, 2 chains. 68 links; "thence. N. 46½° E., 1 chain, 75 links; thence N. 51° E, 2 "chains, 61 links; thence N. 52° E., 2 chains and 90 links, "to a stake; thence N. 64½° E., 4 chains, 6 links, to chest-"nut tree; thence N. 69° E., 2¼ chains, to chestnut stump: "thence S. 66° E., 5 chains, 64 links, to an ash tree; thence "S. 77° E. 4 chains, 86 links, to stake by road that leads "thro' the Neck; thence by the road N. 9° W., 12 chains, "81 links; thence N. 13½° W., 5 chains, 17 links; thence "N. 14½° W., 2 chains, 75 links; thence N. 12½° W., 2 chains, "66 links; thence by the highway that leads to the landing, "W. 8½° S., 6 chains, 75 links; thence W. 17° S., 6 chains, "15 links; thence W. 26° S., 5½ chains; thence on a straight "line to the place we first begin at. Containing 53¾ acres "and 36 rods."

(See History, page 59.)

6—In 1728 the names of Thomas, Tristram and Samuel
appear in the following agreement to change a highway:
Recorded L. 2, p. 97.

"Whereas, When Cow Neck gate-right land was laid
"first out by Samuel Clowes, John Sands and Jonathan
"Smith, and they left four rods wide for a highway there in
"several parts of the Neck, and afterwards the same was
"confirmed by the Commissioners of the Highways, and so
"it lay for many years, and the Inhabitants finding that
"highway was not so convenient as it might be, if it should
"be moved where it would sute the convenience of the nai-
"borhood better, and for that we moved it, and also agreed
"how and where it should be moved; and then they, the
"said Commrs. and required them to move the said high-
"way to run as the Inhabitants had last agreed, and
"accordingly ye said Commissioners did move ye said high-
"way and confirm the same; and ye Commrs. desired
"those men that had their land divided by ye former high-
"way, to take it in, and so to joyne their land together;
"and it pleased the Inhabitants that it should be so, and
"accordingly it hath been done by them. And it now be-
"ing the request of Richard Cornell that he may take up
"his proportionable part of ye said former highway, that is,
"according as it did go throw or joyne to his land; and we
"thinking his request reasonable, we therefore do hereby
"agree and consent to it, provided their is enof of said for-
"mer hieway adjoying to ye said Richard Cornell's land,
"and as an occasion of our assenting and consenting that he
"requests, we have hereunto set our hands this 24th day of
"August, Anno Domini 1728.

Jost Springsteen, Lewis Hewlett,   Adam Mott,
Thomas Dodge, Joseph Thorne,   Joseph Latham,
Calip Cornell,   Richard Place,   Stephen Johnson,
Sam. Sands,   Jasher A. Carman, Joseph Halstead,
Sam. Dodge,   Wm. Huchings,   Hendrickson Ramsay,
Thomas Huchins, Andries Onderdonk, Cornelius Polhemus,
Isam Ramson,   Tristram Dodge, John Allison.

"The above-said highway compared with the original
"and entered by me.

"THOS. GILDERSLEEVE, Clarck."

10—Peter Monfort, Rem Remsen and Cornelius Van Wyck, Executors, etc. of Elbert Monfort, To Jeremiah Dodge.

Deed dated March 31, 1730. Recorded L , 2. p. 416, Consideration. £321, 8s., 1½d. Conveys "northwest part of "above farm, the bounds "whereof being a walnut "tree, which is the Widow "Sutton's north east bounds; "thence north 43 rods, 10 "links to a stake, thence W. "2° S. 215 rods 15 links to highway, thence S. 9° E. 44 "rods by the road, thence to point of beginning, 209 rods "to point of beginning. Containing 57¾ acres and 19 rods." Surveyed by Sam. Willis.

NOTE.—The family traditions state that there were *four* Dodges settled originally at Cow Neck. This Jeremiah Dodge may have been a brother of the first Samuel, and the fourth person referred to in said traditions. His relationship to the others is probably established by the letter of Samuel Dodge, Jr. in page 25 of this, where he is called "Uncle Jeremiah," and allusion is made to his grandson Stephen. (See pages 45 and 46 of History.)

11—Robert Hutchings, etc., to Oliver Baxter.

Deed April 28, 1743. Rec. L, 2., p. 274. Consid. 177 pounds. "One certain mes- "suage, etc. in Cow Neck. "Butted, etc., etc., westerly "by the Bay, northerly by ye road that leads to Dodge's "landing til it comes to a White oak marked on three "sides, being Samuel Dodge's corner tree ; easterly by land "of Samuel Dodge, southerly by land of Daniel Whitehead "to ye Millpond and from his land running ye south side "of ye Millpond and Mill-dam down to ye Bay. Contain- "ing 39 acres. more or less."

The above is noted here on account of its referring to Samuel Dodge's lands, etc., and thus assisting identification. The line between the two farms was part of the "Cow Neck middle line" on Clowes' Map.

12—Richard Cornell, etc., to Wilkie Dodge, Carpenter.	Deed dated Feb. 12, 1746. Consid 5 pounds. (This deed is in the custody of H. M. W. Eastman, Esq., of Roslyn, to whom the writer is indebted for a copy, and for

other favors kindly granted.) "All, etc., messuage or ten-
" ement, etc., at Cow Neck lying on W. side of road that
" runs from Samuel Dodge down the Neck. Bounded east
" by said road till it breast the line between Samuel Dodge
" and Thomas Dodge, whereon their houses now stand, and
" from thence a west course to the Creek; westerly by the
" Creek, and southerly by the road that leads down to the
" landing. Containing half an acre of ground."

This is evidently the lot devised by Wilkie Dodge
to his son Samuel, in his will dated Feb. 13, 1752, and Rec.
Lib. 18, p. 148. (See page 59 of the History, where said
will is given.)

13—   WILL OF SAMUEL DODGE,
(Born Block Island, 1691; died N. Y., 1761.)
" The Last Will and Testament of Samuel Dodge, of
" the City of New York, this 25th day of March, Anno
" Dom., 1761, being of perfect mind and memory, do dis-
" pose of the Worldly Estate wherewith it has pleased God
" to bless me in this life, in the following manner and form:
" Imprimis; I give and bequeath to my loving wife
" Elizabeth, all her wearing apparel, my best bed, and suit-
" able furniture for it, with other conveniences to keep
" house, such as a pot, tea-kettle, tramell, fire-shovel and
" tongs, dishes, etc., with privilege to dwell in my now
" dwelling house, in which room, or two rooms she pleases,
" during the time she remains my widow, with the privi-
" ledge of the Yard, well and kitchen, together with all the
" rent of my house at the East end of my ground, and the
" use of my Negro Wench, Jude, during the above time
" (and afterwards the wench to return to my estate.) The
" above Legacy I give to my widow in lieu of her dowry.
" Item: I give to my son, Jeremiah Dodge, all that
" house and lot of ground situate in New York, fronting
" Queen Street, in Montgomery's ward," [now No. 380
" Pearl St.] " lying between a Lott of Doctor Lawrence on

"the north side, and another Lott belonging and now in the
"possession of myself on the south side; together with that
"house at East end of my Lotts, after the death of my
"widow, to him, his heirs and assigns forever.

"Item: I give to my other son, Samuel Dodge, all
"that house and Lott of ground in the which we both dwell,"
"[now 378 Pearl St.] "adjoining on the north side to the
"above bequeathed house and Lott; on the south side to a
"Lott belonging or now in the possession of Philip Pelton;
"the two above bequeathed Lotts to be equally divided in
"the breadth at the east or rear side of the said houses, with
"a straight line eastward to the rear or east end of all my
"ground, to him, his heirs and assigns forever.

"And I ordain that my two sons, Jeremiah and
"Samuel, (whom I constitute my executors) do equally bear
"the charge of defraying all my just debts, all my moneys
"and wench Jude, after she has served my widow as afore-
"said, to be equally divided between them for that purpose;
"and all my other household goods to be equally divided
"between my two sons and my daughter, Deborah Mott,
"except such goods as are bequeathed to my widow afore-
"said, and after she has done with them, to be Divided as
"above.

"And I also ordain, notwithstanding the above be-
"queathments, that one feather bed, with a single tow
"ticken, two sheets, two pillows and a bolster, a blanket
"and coverled, be given to my granddaughter, Deborah
"Dodge, with ten pounds, when of age or married.

"Item: I give to my grandson, Samuel Dodge, son
"of Wilkie Dodge, deceased, all that ground lying on Cow
"Neck, Long Island, near the house of Joseph Dodge, lying
"the south side of the road that leads from said house up
"the neck between said road, and the fence of Oliver Baxter,
"be it more or less, to him, his heirs and assigns forever.

"And I hereby Disalow, Revoke and Disanull all
"other former Wills, Testaments, Legacies and Executors
"by me before this time named, Willed and bequeathed.
"Ratifying and confirming this and no other, to be my last
"Will and Testament.

In testimony whereof, I have hereunto set my hand and seal the day and year above written.

SAM'L DODGE.   [L. S.]

Witnesses:

Philip Pelton,
Vinsent Montanje.
Robert North.

1576612

Proved, etc., May 23, 1761.

Recorded New York Surrogate office, Liber 23, page 28."
(See page 60 of History.)

14—Copy of letter of Samuel Dodge, Jr., son of the preceding testator, addressed to Thomas Dodge, Jr., son of the first Thomas.

NEW YORK, June 16, 1776.

LOVING COUSIN:

I rec'd a letter from you before I left home in which you Desired me to Search my father's Writings in relation to Some Difficulties respecting the line between the two farms —— I have Searched accordingly, and find one or two old deeds or Quit claims from your father, but they respected Some of the upper fields, but I cannot find a word about the line in Question; 'tis unaccountable to me how the line came to be given Straight; I well remember the turn at the head of the great hollow. I suppose the land was Surveyed to Uncle Tristram, and if the Surveyer was directed to keep the fence in runing the line (as doubtlefs he was), then it's Strange he did not Draw the Deed Accordingly; for Sure I am the fence was never Strait Since I can remember: the miftake muft have happened Either Wilfully or thro inadvertancy; I advife the parties Concerned to compare the deed With the Surveyer's field book; if Willifs was the man perhaps he may give fome light in the matter and tell how it happen'd —— in the meantime, if I by further Searching can find anything relating to it Shant fail to let you know it; but I don't expect I Shall. for I guefs it was a miftake in Writing the deed you Mention; and if Such it ought to be rectify'd if it can be done by the prefent pofsefsers giving Quit claims to each other of all lands beyond the fence, or otherwife, as they can agree—if my father has Sold more land than he ought to have done, and that Defignedly (Which I hardly think is the cafe), then the damage muft be made good by his heirs——I saw and talk'd with your Son at poughkeepsie yefterday week, he was well and hearty; if you see any of Uncle Jeremiah's family, pleafe to remember me to them, and tell him I faw his grandfon, Stephen, at Fort Montgomery laft Wednesday; he was very well and faid he had lately heard from home, that they were all well; he is again in Capt. Rofekrans's Company; as for news in town, altho there is a great deal of talk, and news and preparations to receive the expected fleet, yet I Suppofe I cannot inform you of anything but What you will other ways hear of befor you receive this.

I reft with much refpect, Your loving Coufin,

SAM'L DODGE.

This letter is important as referring to "Uncle Jeremiah," who must therefore have been a brother of the first Samuel, and probably the owner of the farm deeded in 1730 from Monfort Estate to Jeremiah Dodge; also the father of

Tristram Dodge, mentioned on pages 44, 45 and 59 of
History, and the grandfather of Stephen Dodge, who
afterwards emigrated to Nova Scotia.

A corroboration of this theory is found on page 45, line
17 of the History, where it is stated that Tristram was a
descendant of the "early settlers of Cow Bay."

The following two conveyances are given as completing
the area of the Dodge lands on the south east corner,
though not so ancient as the preceding ones.

15—Sarah Rapelye et al. Deed dated Apr. 18, 1810. Rec.
to L. 129 page 217. Consid,
Trustram Dodge, of $1,287.50. (The grantee is
Cow Neck. probably a son of Joseph
  Dodge and grandson of Tristram.) "All, &c., part of
Tract which Daniel Rapelye purchased of Robert Sutton.
Begin at S. W. corner thereof, and at S. E. corner of farm
of John Hegeman, thence by land of said Hegeman, Minne
and Peter Onderdonk, N. 4¼° W., 16 chains, where it meets
the land of Obadiah DeMilt; thence by lands of said De
Milt, N. 85° E., 35 chains, to a forked oak tree standing
at the edge of a bank adjoining Hempstead Harbor:
thence down the bank to Hempstead Harbor; thence
along the shore of Hempstead Harbor, S. 24¼° E., 11
chains, 22 links; thence up the bank to an oak tree
standing near the bank; thence by other lands which were
of Daniel Rapelye, N. 84¾° W., 6 chains, 35 links, to a
marked birch sapling; thence S. 79° W., crossing a road
leading through the woods to the shore aforesaid, 2 chains;
thence along north side of said road N. 89° W., 4 chains, 16
links; thence along north side of said road N. 76¼° W., 1
chain, 78 links; thence S., 89½° W., 2 chains, 92 links, along
by said road; thence S. 85° W., 4½ chains, to a stake; thence
along other lands of Daniel Rapelye, S. 6 chains, 10 links:
thence S., 82° W., 16½ chains, to place of beginning. Containing 44½ acres.

With liberty for Tristram Dodge to pass over said road
to and from cleared land and likewise through other land of
Estate of D. Rapelye, along north side thereof adjoining
land of John Hegeman till it comes to land of Wm. Salts;
and then likewise to pass through land of Wm. Salts as

same were reserved by Robert Sutton and sold to Daniel Rapelye to and from the main road leading through the middle of Cow Neck."

| 16—Henry Coutant, of Cow Neck, and wife, to John Dodge, of Cow Neck.. | Deed dated Sept. 10, 1793. Rec. L. 4, p. 319. Consid. 220 pounds. Conveys 18 acres and 30 rods on East side of Cow Neck. Bounded, etc. "Beginning at |

"the North East corner of Tunis Bogart's land, thence running westerly in a straight line by said Bogart to a Stone Fence, thence Northerly along said fence by Rapelye's land to locust tree, thence Easterly to black oak sapling on the bank and so the same course to highwater mark ; thence Southerly along the beach to place of beginning."

This same plot of 18 acres and 30 rods was sold by John Dodge and Hannah, his wife, to Israel Pearsall, of Hempstead Harbor, by deed dated in April, 1795, and recorded in Liber 4, page 322. It is probably the small tract in the extreme south-easterly corner of the Dodge lands, as shown on the map on page 13.

The foregoing conveyances and other papers, together with the map, will show very clearly where the original farms were situated. They covered a compact area of about 630 acres, or very nearly one square mile, running from Cow Bay to Hempstead Harbor, with the exception of the "20 acre lot" of the Onderdonk family, which is surrounded on all sides by the Dodge lands An attempt was made to trace the conveyances of each parcel of land down to the present owners, (1896) but this undertaking has, for the present, been abandoned, since many of the ancient deeds were never placed on record. The following incomplete list of the various owners is, however, given, as it may possibly be found of some use.

The homestead farm of Thomas Dodge is still in possession of his family, in the person of his great grandson, Henry Onderdonk Dodge, at the ripe old age of 90 years, to whom and to his son. Henry Thomas Dodge, the writer is greatly indebted for facilities and information furnished. As stated on page 233 of the History, this "unbroken possession

"of near two hundred years in their ancient house, that has
"tranquilly looked upon the convulsive struggles of this
"long period, is an extraordinary example of constancy in
"ancient footprints; during centuries that have witnessed
"the ceaseless movement of nations into new lands, and their
"transformation in laws, customs and manners."

The other lands owned by Thomas Dodge passed to his
sons Amos and William; to Mary Cornell, Daniel Hoag-
land, John S. Burtis, James Udall, Wm. B. Miles and others;
and finally, partly to Mrs. Smull, and partly to W. Bourke
Cockran.

The farm of Tristram descended to his son Joseph, by
his will, dated Oct. 20, 1760, proved Dec. 29, 1760, recorded
in N. Y. Surr., Lib. 22, p. 313; from Joseph to his son,
Isaac H., by deed dated June 30, 1809, and recorded in Lib.
73, page 283; from Isaac H. Dodge to Richard Mott, by
deed dated May 1, 1871, recorded in Liber 346, page 19,
consideration $20,500, being 79 acres by estimation. Rich-
ard Mott conveyed to Jesse H. Bunnell, the present owner,
by deed dated Oct. 5, 1880, recorded Lib. 689, page 439,
consideration $17,500, same 79 acres. The fine old family
residence is in the southeasterly corner of the property, near
the shore of Hempstead Harbor, opposite Sea Cliff, L. I.

Both of the tracts of Samuel Dodge, on the Sandy Hollow road, passed through the hands, among others, of Wm.
H. Salt, Rhoda and Catharine Hegeman, John S. Burtis,
etc., etc. They were recently conveyed by George Brown
to his daughter, Fanny T. Brown, by deed dated April 24,
1894, and recorded in Liber 1020, page 113.

The plot belonging to Samuel Dodge, east of the Thomas
Dodge homestead farm, and the ten acre lot south of said
plot, were afterwards in possession of Walter J. Cornell,
Obadiah DeMilt, George Willis, James Udall, Wm. B.
Miles and others, and were finally acquired by W. B. Cockran, at the same time that he purchased the easterly portion
of the Thomas Dodge property.

The above record is confessedly very incomplete. At a
future time further investigations may be made, and the re-
sults given to those interested in our family antiquities.

Part III.--Reminiscences of the Dodge Homestead at Port Washington, by Henry Thomas Dodge.

The location of the house seems to have been determined by the proximity of the "Old Indian Spring" immediately in front of it, and on the edge of the mill-pond, formerly the Cove. The cellar was first dug where the garden now is, but the next morning about six inches of water being found in it, a new one was dug further up the hill, in a dryer spot. This was early in 1700.

The south end of the house (always called "the shop") was used for weaving, there being a loom there. Thomas, the brother of Henry O. Dodge, was a weaver by trade. In this room, during the Revolutionary war, twelve Hessians were stationed all one winter.

The "Indian Spring" was walled up by the Dodges, as now in use. The present aged beech tree that overhangs it is of peculiar, low spreading shape, on account of cutting off the top branches, so that the fine view from the house windows should not be obstructed. Its bark is covered with initials, cut in; the oldest inscription is T. D., 1807, being my uncle Thomas, above mentioned. There are in addition, among others, H. D., 1820, M. W. D., 1858, and H. T. D., 1867, being the initials of my father, my brother, and myself. There were formerly two great weeping willows near the spring, together with a large stone, shaped like a seat, where my grandfather used to sit in their shade. They were both blown down about 1860 in a storm.

There is now standing by the roadside, about one hundred feet north of the house, what was once a noble specimen of a pine tree, but which is now dead, supposed to have been killed by lightning a few years ago. This tree, in the year 1825, when it was not much larger than a man's arm, was transplanted by my grandfather, aided by his sons Robert, Peter and Henry, from his "big woods," adjoining Hempstead Harbor, to its present position, where for many years it has served as one of the ranges used by pilots in entering the harbor of Port Washington.

My great grandfather, Thomas (son of the first Thomas), was a subscriber to a copy of the Laws of New York, from Nov. 11, 1752, to May 22, 1762, published in the latter year.

The name of Abraham Polhemus also appears as a subscriber, who was probably an ancestor of my wife. This copy is now in my possession, in very good condition.

Adam Mott, a neighbor, was a sea-captain in the old days, and once he brought a cargo of what was represented to be gunpowder, to be stored in the house, over the weaving room. It remained there two or three days, and for the privilege thus granted he invited the said Thomas aboard of his vessel, and presented him with a chest filled with flasks of good Holland gin. The chest and some of the empty flasks are still in the house, but the gin has disappeared.

My grandfather, William Dodge, sailed two packets from this place to New York, and was in the habit of anchoring them in Dodge's Creek, below the house, at Dodge's landing (before the mill-dam was built.) There were then five feet of water at high tide, while now the depth is not two feet. Dodge's Pond was formed in 1795, by Caleb Cornell building a dam across the mouth of the former creek or cove.

At one time, during the Revolution, Wm. Dodge lost some sheep, and on going up into the lot to look for them, on walking from the brow of the hill, down into the locusts, or "little woods," he espied there two English soldiers, who had killed the sheep and had them hung up and partly dressed, being still at work upon them when he saw them. He walked away, not daring to say a word, and came down to the house, knowing the futility of a remonstrance on his part.

In the "hard winter" of 1780, some relatives came from the west side of Tappan Zee on the ice, across the mainland on the snow, and over the Sound on the ice ; made a visit of two days and nights at this place, and returned in the same way.

In the days of Slavery there would be hauled into the old kitchen fire-place big back-logs, so large that two slaves could sit on each end—four in all—without crowding. In front of the fire-place my grandmother and my great-grandmother before her, baked cakes in an old oven, which is still in the house. One day one of the slaves (Greetje by name) reported that while she was looking for eggs, she had seen a little red dog in the old Dutch thatched barn on the north side of the hill, close to the homestead, up the farm lane, or

the flat near the big black walnut tree. Shortly afterwards the poultry began to disappear mysteriously, so a trap was set, and Mr. Fox was evolved from the little red dog.

In 1808 my grandfather, finding that the roof of this old barn, after a heavy storm, had leaked down upon the horses, determined to build a new one. My father remembers the erection of said barn, he being three years old at the time. It was built by Joel Davis, my grandfather's first son-in-law, who married my aunt, Sarah Dodge, and always claimed that he took the daughter in payment for building the barn. Dr. Chapman was present at the raising in case of accident, which, however, did not occur. He was of great assistance on the occasion in other ways. One hundred people, small and great, were present. The raising and the dinner were all over by one o'clock, and the rest of the day was spent in playing ball in the orchard, right above the new barn. In those days deer were not infrequently seen in and near the cattle-yard. The "new barn" is still in use.

On the former property of Samuel Dodge, on the northeast corner of the Sandy Hollow road and the present Flower Hill avenue, a well was once dug seventy-six feet deep, reaching creek mud and clam shells at the bottom, as witnessed by my father who was present. This shows the depth of the glacial drift at that spot.

The wood-pile formerly stood right in front of the homestead, and my grandfather would say that not until forty loads of wood was piled up there, did he consider that he had his winter supply on hand.

On the 16th of March, 1805, he was appointed by Gov. Morgan Lewis, to the office of Coroner for Queens County, his appointment being still preserved in good order in the family archives. At one time he and Thomas Thorne, of "Success" went to Albany on horseback, on official business and returned the same way, a decided contrast to the present mode of travel. He was one of the deacons or trustees of the Reformed Dutch Church at Manhasset, when first built, after it was removed from "Success." He and his sister Molly would ride to church in the farm wagon on chairs, in which they also sat during service—one of the chairs is still extant in the household.

During the war of 1812 my Uncles Robert and Thomas were stationed at Fort Greene, in Brooklyn. My father was relieved of military duty on account of a certificate from Dr. Townsend, that his shoulder was liable to dislocation. My uncle Peter, who lived then in New York, was in the habit of riding to the training ground at Manhasset, over the ferries and through all the tollgates free of charge when in uniform.

Among the family papers is a regimental warrant dated August 18, 1817, and signed by M. Townsend, Lt. Col., appointing my Uncle, Thomas Dodge, a Corporal, "in Capt. Martin Rapylee's Company" in the 17th Regiment, New York State Militia.

During the Civil war, my brother, Jordan C. Dodge, was drafted in 1863, and paid $300 exemption money. Alonzo P. Dodge, son of Uncle Peter, enlisted in the Navy during three years of the war and returned in safety to his home after doing good service.

The Following is a List of Some of the Relics Etc., at the Homestead.

One Indian axehead, of hard grey sandstone, nine inches long, five and a quarter pounds weight.

One Indian mortar of stone for grinding corn, etc., height six inches, inside width six inches, depth, one and three-quarter inches.

One Indian mortar of hard wood, hollowed by fire from tree trunk, height thirty inches, inside width, fourteen inches, depth, seventeen and one-half inches.

One cannon ball three and one-half inches in diameter, six and a quarter pounds weight, left by the Hessians.

One ancient oak checker board, two inches square.

One pair wafer-irons with my great grandfathers initials T. D., 1762 on one side, and his wife's initials, S. D., on the other.

Also horse pistols and other firearms, swords, etc., etc., such as are frequently found in old Colonial houses.

---

www.ingramcontent.com/pod-product-compliance
Lightning Source LLC
Chambersburg PA
CBHW021638270326
41931CB00008B/1065